Kathy,

Good or Evil... right or anyone have the ability far would you travel, w... .... y.. ....me, What trials and tribulations would you face to be with the only person you've loved... your soul mate... created for you, by the very hands of God?

As you read the following pages, try to understand the characters, their love for each other, and the sacrifices they make... just to simply love one another.

A Collection of Fantastic and Heartfelt Poems: Volume I

Best regards,

By

Wayne Fieldhouse

12/5/06

ISBN: 0-7596-3457-2 (e-book)
ISBN: 1-4107-7905-X (Paperback)

This book is printed on acid free paper.

Cover concept by Wayne Fieldhouse
Cover design by James Haven, jhaven007@excite.com

1stBooks - rev. 10/29/03

Dedication

Many cultures believe in guardian angels. I never used to, but all of that has changed. For many years, my heart had been cold, but through your light, wisdom, and understanding, a miserable wretch became a man. Without the Angel, there can be no Heretic. I'd like to dedicate this book to you, my inspiration, muse, and redeemer.

My Father had told me years ago that his children were his greatest teachers, but I never thought I would learn so much, in such little time. I've been so very blessed with two beautiful children – two children that have helped uncover an inner child that had been buried in rubble for so many years. I would like to dedicate "My Little Girl" to my daughter, Ashley and "Making the Man" to my son, Ryan. It's through my children that I find my hope and through my wife that I find my strength.

I'd like to thank my wife for her support and patience with me when I write. Not many people know this, but the "Heretic" series almost ended three times. She knows the characters are an integral part of me and simply smiles when I tell her I have written yet another poem about the Heretic and the Angel. She believes that I will write the next "Great American Novel." For that – and for too many reasons to list – I'll always love her.

About the Book

This collection of poetry presents an interwoven and epic tapestry of romance, religion, and philosophy in a world of true fantasy. In the first part of the book, the protagonist Heretic searches for his kindred spirit, but paradoxically discovers God has forbidden their pre-destined love. Come, look at the world through his eyes, feel his heart's pain, and try to understand the workings of his mind. Will the Heretic ever find peace?

The second section of the book is a small collection of heartfelt poems, taken from various influences in the author's life, along with a few teasers from what may be the second installment of the Heretic's epic.

Journey with the poet through these pages into another world, perhaps a world not so different from your own.

Table of Contents

Part I

The Heretic and the Angel: From Darkness to Light

The Edge of Reality 1
The Time has Come 3
Vociferation of My Soul 5
"Ø" 7
The Bridge of Discrimination 9
When My Angel Cries 11
The Day that God Died 13
Phantasm 16
Culmination: The Cleansing of Souls 19

Part II

In Her Eyes 26
My Little Girl 27
Making the Man 29
Kindred Spirits 30
Dreams in the Darkness 32
A Time Long Since Forgotten 36
I am the Vine… 45

Part I

The Heretic and the Angel: From Darkness to Light

The Edge of Reality

The edge of reality,
Is a conundrum that perplexes me

Some say space and time were born,
Others hypothesize in haste and scorn

However you incline the way it begins,
Vagabond men roamed the earth with repugnant sin

Perhaps millions of years ago my soul began,
To futilely repeat itself until I become a man

Perhaps it began in the time of chivalry, pestilence, and cunning,
Perchance it spawned in the dawning age of milk and honey

As the cogs of time gyrate about,
No one can hear my soul when it cries out

Days turn to months, months to years,
Trudging through my existence,
My mental anguish falls on deaf ears

The agony, the ecstasy,
My apostasy is controlling me,
Dear God why can't you hear my pleas?

As if by fate, one peculiar day
An Angel was sent my way

Hair of gold, emeralds for eyes,
Dear God why have you brought her to me?
It is inevitable she will gaze despitefully,
She knows nothing of my contemptuous lies

Wayne Fieldhouse

My fractured soul how will it heal?
I gaze upon her with such delighted zeal

The body of a goddess, inexplicable by tongue,
And still her soul amazingly surpasses,
My paradoxical being for once feeling young,
How could such a wretch incur her eyes from the masses?

Her scintillating form comes my way,
My tongue has been taken, no words can I say

Near her undraped bosom I can see,
A necklace made of diamond, cradling a key

She puts it in her hand,
Then to my heart,
No longer can I stand

The darkness around me flees my presence,
My enigmatic existence filled with acquiescence

The edge of reality now seems mundane,
My curse finally lifted, human again,
Perhaps this was in God's master plan,
The agony forsaken,
You have made me that man

The Time has Come

The time has come to pay the price,
Inimical deities with infinite strife

Armageddon has finally begun,
The universe's infinite web is undone

The forces of Darkness and the forces Light,
Clash at the River Styx for the paramount prize

Adjudication of an Angel's soul,
Her existence snared by a beguiling troll

Osiris and Enubis await your disembarkation,
God save your soul, I'll see to your salvation

Looking back, when you first entered my ambivalent domain,
I knew at that moment I would no longer be the same

Your presence was now taken from me,
I felt helpless, filled with rage and animosity

How could this troll have filled you with this bane,
For his sins I would drive him insane

A Gordian knot for me to undo,
My love for my Angel is so very true

How I longed for your kiss and tender embrace,
How I longed to caress your resplendent face

To have you at my side to hold,
To warm my heart now so cold

My mind confounded, my soul in defenestration,
Dear God, why this damnation?

Wayne Fieldhouse

Titan Prometheus hear my plea,
Come to Hades and set her free

Athena....Solomon bestow thy wisdom
I implore you both, give her back her freedom

I will pay you whatever the fee,
Even if it would have to be me

My soul for hers, an even trade,
I demand that such a pact be made

Then my Angel was set free,
The chains of Prometheus no longer be

A penitent sacrifice I am willing to make,
There is no reason for God to forsake

The time has come for you to realize,
My love for you is as endless as time

Vociferation of My Soul

The vociferation of a wretched man's soul,
Can only be heard by his guardian angel,
Who succors in the ultimate toll

An even trade was made at last,
My Angel was extricated,
But what of our past

It was always a forbidden love,
That between raven and a dove

My spirit increased in its declension,
The pact was made with the god of Hades,
His twisted form of prognostication

My downward spiral through the stratum of Hell,
Virgil was now my guide,
I prayed only that my Angel was well

His attempts to save my soul were in vain,
He stopped not the demons from raping my soul,
I'd never felt such anguish, such pain

My spirit stripped, what was happening, I didn't know,
There I stood in endless vertigo

Then the Sirens cried out to me,
I cannot move, where is my Angel?
For the love of God set me free!

Circe, for Christ's sake where are you now?
This can't be happening to me,
Let me out!

Wayne Fieldhouse

The Siren then had her way,
I betrayed my Angel; I must live in shame

She had fallen from heaven to be with me,
She now knows the truth,
A fuckin' wretch I shall forever be

All of my life, never to be forgiven,
Without my Angel, life wasn't worth living,
From that day forward I would be known as Griffin

"Ø"

As I languidly trudge through the labyrinthine corridors of my mind,
I've come to discern something that was left behind

As I peer through the mirror, I gaze and abhor,
Who is this man I see behind those eyes,
Is he trying to escape my soul,
Or does wish to enter…who led him to the door?

The door that leads to my fractured, frayed soul,
An amorphous pool filled with flagitious zeal,
The place that desiderates to collect the absolute toll,
The presence that lives to kill

Until now he has been locked away,
Once imprisoned, but knowing he'd be released one day

His essence is filled with a sanguine addiction,
To rape, to pillage, to maim, to take what is his,
All vile and repugnant affliction

An indelible mark that cannot be cleansed,
What of the other…he's surely come to his end

A tribulation has begun,
They can no longer coincide,
There can be only one!

The vacillation can no longer endure,
I now grow weary,
Make him stop, dear God I implore

If set free, his bane will disseminate,
All will perish; no one is safe

Wayne Fieldhouse

There has been only one who can extinguish his sovereign rage,
His Angel; her love acted as his impervious cage

Now with her fading presence,
Unknowingly she has started his acquiescence

It's sad to find even I cannot tell,
Will she be in time to quiet, to stifle, to quell?

This Heretic prays that she notices soon,
For if she doesn't, the result is certain doom

Dear God it's hard to see,
What I've become…what's become of me?

The Bridge of Discrimination

As I watch the sky turn gray, my apostasy the host,
The future is forsaken,
No turning back; I must now pay the cost,
As I approach the Bridge of Discrimination

My surroundings are cold and pale
The bridge is made of steel,
Screams fill the air,
Alone, I drop and kneel

Deafening silence pierces my brain,
Dear God why won't you just kill me,
I now realize my atonement can never be made

A myriad of demons appear,
To feed on the remnants of my soul,
I show no emotion, not even fear,
I've given up all hope

Shackled to this bridge by my sins,
A clap of thunder cracks in the distance,
I guess the other wins

As I look up into this morose sky,
Only Cassiopeia I see,
Is it my day to die?
Where is my Angel?
The only one who can grant me life eternally

Radburn rain begins to descend,
In a final effort I beckon your name,
I sense what is coming; it is my end

Wayne Fieldhouse

A bright flash fills the Lungs of Hell,
It looks like a Phoenix, dear God I've gone blind,
Who is there I cannot tell

Samael?, Michael?, Azrael?, I demand to know who is there
I feel something touching my lips to silence,
I hear a beautiful voice, "It's someone who cares"

I feel secure cradled in this being's wing
What the hell is happening?
I'm unsure
The queerest sense of agony and ecstasy,
I've been restored

As I awaken I see my Angel by my side,
Is this a cruel joke?
I must be out of my mind

I lay awake to watch her breathing,
Then trace her ethereal silhouette,
I quickly rise and scream, "This isn't real I'm..."

My Angel rises, puts her index finger to her lips to quell,
Dear God, it was you with me in Hell

I look in the mirror and see my left eye,
The indelible mark has been moved,
How can she ever believe me again; my lies

She said, "The mark has been moved so now you can see,
All has been forgiven,
This will be a daily reminder of the pain you have caused, especially
    to me,
But you will no longer be known as Griffin"

I drop to my knees and tell her, "I'm so sorry for your sorrow,
If you remember only one thing,
My love for you grows stronger with every passing moment,
But I can never love you more than tomorrow"

10

When My Angel Cries

It feels as though an eternity has passed since my servitude in Hell,
My Angel had saved my soul, alleviated my spell

Satan was angered by her intervention,
I assumed he felt it was some sort of insurrection

The lord of Hades made a pact with God,
"Let me test their faith in you and their love",
Deus agreed with a gentle nod

The presence of God left my Angel, striking her with madness,
The pain was insurmountable,
Leaving her with boundless sadness

"What has happened to me, what have I done?
Why did God leave us,
Just when our lives together had begun?"

I summoned the Lord through incantations,
"Why have you banished her, she has been a worthy anchorite!"
There was no answer; I lay awake that night

In a dream the Lord appeared to me, I'm sure,
He told me, "Sometimes to see the light, you must suffer for the cure"

I watched my Angel sleep, then she despondently began to cry,
At that moment I felt a piece of my soul actually die

Morning broke, saw my Angel awaken,
She had a vacant look in her eyes,
As if her memory had been taken

"Don't you remember who I am?"
"Keep your distance if you'd like to keep your life young man!"

"Cronus…you bastard, what have you done?
Don't you know who I am…what I'm capable of?
I am not Jacob and shall not fall,
I will see to your death…and put an end to you once and for all"

"Heretic…be sure not to cross my path,
For if you do, the result shall be my wrath"

The Lord spoke and said, "Mephistopheles…this now comes to an
    end,
It is obvious that this man would die for his Angel,
And evident that their love will always transcend"

"Celeste, the only thing I ask of you,
Is to look into his eyes and have no doubt that his love for you is true

Know that you are two kindred spirits, who function only as a whole,
Forever interwoven in space and time, by the existence of your soul"

I looked into my Angel's eyes, "Don't you see it was nothing but a
    test",
She gazed into my soul, "What else could it have been, my darling
    Orpheus"

Now that I see there was no real pact,
There is no turning back

I professed my undying love for her and held her tight,
"I promised you this scourge would end my love, quick as day turns
    to night"

The Day that God Died

Seven years, seven months, and seven days have passed since the
    curse,
Even with God's grace she has not fully recovered,
It appears everything has taken a turn for the worst

My Angel lies upon my threshing floor,
Looking lifeless, crippled, and pale,
Unable to move is she anymore,
How can this be the end of our tale?

I invoke the Lord's name and curse him again,
"If you will not help us, perhaps I can release her pain"

"Heretic, you pretentious fool,
Don't you see that this is not about you?"

The Heretic spread his body o'er hers,
"You inane bastard, your body can't absorb the curse,
Your necrotic soul can't assimilate such incredible force,
There is nothing you can do; she used up her energy source"

"I summon my brother Elijah and all of his power,
I will drive these demons from your soul and see them cower"

A most pallid light began to emanate,
The Heretic opened his eyes and lay aghast at the Angel he saw,
The Lord spoke and said, "I'm sorry…this was her fate"

In a timid voice he told of watching her from the dawn of time,
Only together could they achieve the perfect paradigm

For seven days rain from the heavens descended,
His Angel was no more…she was DEAD!

"The purpose of this I do not see,
She was to be my wife, but instead my heart carries an elegy"

The Lord spoke and said, "This is what you get for a soul that is so
        meriting,
You would never be worthy of such an unadulterated mate,
You've been nothing to her but a scorpion's sting,
Pathetic fool…you've fallen short once again, you're too late!"

The Heretic was astonished at what the Lord said,
He catatonically stares at God, in his silent reverie,
The words he simply could not comprehend

Just at that moment the metamorphosis began,
His shopworn heart broken as he wailed in disbelief,
This was the catalyst for his soul's cleave

Good versus evil no longer exists,
The vacillation has ceased,
The Heretic began to speak in tongue,
God has freed the taste of death that had always lived within

The Heretic's frail body convulsed violently,
"What have you done?! What's happening to me?!"

The Heretic stared blankly at the blue moon,
His crystalline talisman fell from his neck to shatter,
"You imbecile…you've sealed your doom",
"I have no purpose now…you no longer matter!"

"Jehovah, come kneel before your new Master,
Wait, better yet…why don't you crawl,
Infidel….how dare you turn around, you bastard,
I am known as Dahak, your servants called me Baal"

"You saw the fear I cast in the Olympian's eyes,
It is now your turn, you crass shit…it's your day to die"

The Heretic and God battled at great length,
The Heretic was winning, God was faltering in strength

The Heretic conjures his mighty lyre and played a dissonant chord,
The Lord's eardrums shattered as he hit the floor

The cacophonous sound resonated and the heavens began to fall,
The Heretic sat and watched the blood soaked winged angels descend
    to the River Styx,
Maniacal laughter emerged from his gullet, as they listened to Ktulu's
    Call

The chord he played had such incredible power,
There was silence in the heavens for about half an hour

Seven angels played a requiem on seven horns,
The heavens froze over, the Heretic no longer felt scorned

He kissed his fallen Master on the head and asked, "Why the
    mendacity, all of your lies?"
The Heretic stepped upon an ice floe and his tortured soul lit a flame
    in his funeral pyre,
This was the day...THE DAY THAT GOD DIED!

Phantasm

The fabric of space and time are undone,
He has returned, the forgotten son

Born only to die, but cursed to eternally live,
His agnostic nature will never let him forgive

His destiny was to futilely relive his life,
To battle the forces of darkness in his soul,
Until he once again found his lost wife

Reborn again, the Heretic is alive,
To feel nothing but disquiet,
His senseless existence is but a lie

Against himself he wages war,
Never to enjoy the simplicity of life,
To always feel contempt and abhor

The symphony won't leave his head,
The voices must stop, or soon he'll be dead

The modern Prometheus has sealed his doom,
A loveless existence, filled with sempiternal gloom

Expect no sympathy, there's none to be had,
To live his life without his Angel's love,
Dear God he's going mad

Until he met his Angel, his life was incomplete,
Not knowing that she ever existed and God had lay dead at his feet

Unaware of his past,
His restless soul searched for peace…
Dear God…peace at last

His soul eclipsed by this perpetual decadence,
He hadn't much time; there was only one chance

The Heretic lifted his head to study the blue moon,
At that moment the phantasm appeared...who in God's name are
    you?

Vaguely familiar he searched his heart and simply stared,
"You were once my love, the one for whom I've always cared"

The Heretic gazed at Plato's true form in quandary,
"This is not true...this cannot be!"

The Angel reached over to give a thornless white and tea rose to her
    fallen master,
The memories came back like a raging eagre,
His feeble mind fell to the pain, the guilt and failure,
He collapsed as blood deluges from his eyes, faster and faster

The sky turned black as all reality vermiculated,
Now there was no space...no time,
The Heretic rose and transmogrified to the man he most hated

In this surreal world the Angel began to speak,
"You lost your focus in life, your drive,
I felt this was your only chance to survive"

"Your punishment for insurgency was never to know our love,
I saw you suffering and I could no longer wait,
Against the laws of the universe I had to come"

At that moment the Chimera appeared,
"Insolent women, you know this is verboten",
The Angel spoke, "Just as I feared",
"You should have left him for dead, and forgotten"

The Heretic spoke, "Impertinent bastard leave my wife be,
Or I shall torment your soul for all eternity"

Wayne Fieldhouse

The Chimera assigned only one way to win,
Roll the bones for his wife and redemption of sin

The Heretic agreed as the fallen angels he had slain, sat at his side,
Each turned their head and cursed him with their eye

As he rolled the bones he noticed his talisman was now an albatross,
He ululated, "No, I was tricked…I have lost!"

The Chimera fled with his Angel in hand,
"I will hunt this demon until I can no longer stand"

"I summon my brother Bellerophon, Pegasus, and their courage,
I will bring back my wife and our lives will once again flourish"

The battle lasted what to us would be a thousand eternities,
He would not give up, "She will be mine…we will be free"
The mighty Pegasus began to stumble,
The Heretic was thrown from his back,
The universe was again upset with a mighty rumble

The Heretic fell to earth faster and faster; it was only a matter of time,
He lay on his back, near lifeless, crippled, and blind

At the top of his lungs he screamed,
"Remember my love for you is incessant,
In some shape or form…together we shall always be!"

His Angel threw the roses upon the Heretic's remains,
Their petals now drenched red in his blood
"We shall be victorious my beloved…until we meet again"

Culmination: The Cleansing of Souls

The Heretic, drenched in his blood, on the ground did lie,
The Lord looked down upon this weary soul and began to cry

At his near dead body, the Southern Witches gathered 'round,
One spoke and said, "The king of all Heretics, here is your crown"

Mocking him, they placed upon him a crown of thorns,
Unable to do anything, unable to summon his rage, his scorn

At that moment, down the hand of God came,
"I now understand your anguish, my son, rise again"

With crown of thorns, his frail carrion began to levitate,
With his own blood dripping from forehead and face

His eyes now wide open, realizing what must be done,
He had been called by the Lord; he is the only one

Suddenly his wrists and ankles writhed in pain,
His back was whipped, and side began to bleed,
The Lord said, "This must happen once again,"
The Heretic cried so loud it reached Heaven, "Why me?"

The Heretic's decaying body was now restored,
"I must find my Angel and rid this world of the Chimera's scorn"

At the Southern Witches he now peered,
"Where is the one you call Master?"
One by one they fell to the earth and bowed, each one faster,
Pointed to the church near the High Places, trembling, they feared

The Heretic saw the church approach in the distance,
An altered presence he began to perceive,
"I sense that he is hiding from me, this time I will not be deceived"

Wayne Fieldhouse

The Heretic penetrated the church's gates,
Not knowing what to expect, or how God may have twisted his fate

To his surprise, he saw his Angel hung like Saint Peter,
She lay almost lifeless upon the inverted cross,
He had badly beaten her

Then out of the darkness, the Chimera did call,
Pain and suffering he brought to them all,
Away the Angel hid her head,
To avoid watching the dance of the living dead

The Chimera's automaton minions toward the Heretic did lurch,
He then realized that this was not a House of God,
It had brought his Angel to Set's church

Lurking in the shadows the Chimera once again speaks,
"You must now go through your final temptation,
I can tell that you are still weak"

"You must slit your Angel's throat with this scythe",
The Heretic tried to resist his call with all his might

"In you, I'll maim the silence,
Summon your pain, disappointment, and violence"

His eyes now changed to the shade of the stigma in his left eye,
"Dear God what is happening….*by my hand she must die?!*"
*"For all of the pain and suffering you have caused me,
This is my true retribution, your death will set me free"*

The insidious beast emerged from the shadows and cried,
"Do it now you pathetic fool",
The Heretic turned and put finger to lips…silence filled the skies

Dropping the scythe he stated, "To God I have turned my eyes and
    ears,
This was the true reason for my deepest fears,
You see, I killed God from the very start,
I was foolish and never let him enter my heart,
Now on this day you must feel my anguish and pain,
Just as God has realized, but you will feel it on a physical plane"

The Heretic snatched the Chimera and began to speak,
"In the name of the Lord our God, I cast you out unclean spirits,
Christ commands this by the sign of this holy cross I wear,
The power of Christ compels you, the Heretic's schismatic soul must
    now tear!"

With the Chimera in his grasp,
There was a deafening silence,
The Heretic suddenly gasped

"Trifle magician, realize that you have been forsaken by your God"
The Heretic looked into the sky and said, "I will repay my debt
    whatever the cost"

Hit by a bolt of lightning, the Heretic's soul physically cleaved,
The white side of his soul remained in his body,
As they saw the dark side leave

The Chimera hit the floor convulsing in agony,
The Heretic attempted to regain his balance,
"I will now be known as the Hieratic, I am finally free"

The Chimera emerged from the floor, scythe in hand,
"Imbecile do you know what you have done, do you understand?"

Before his eyes the Chimera morphed into his alter ego,
The Hieratic stood in awe and gaped at the evil form clad in black,
The Heretic struck the Hieratic and his Angel he attacked

The Angel lay on her cross staring at the Hieratic with open eyes,
He gazed upon his impious brother; and did despise

Wayne Fieldhouse

With his hand he enacted a gentle gesture,
A myriad of silver spikes came forth,
Piercing the Chimera against the wall,
"There you will stay for eternity to fester"

The Hieratic levitates to his Angel's remains,
To his dismay, he was late once again

Telekinetically he drew spikes from her wrists and ankles and set her
    on the floor,
He attempted to summon his rage, but could find it no more

The Hieratic sat in total disbelief,
"I cannot go through this again,
Dear God the grief"

The ullage that had once been his soul was growing at a cancerous
    rate,
But his melancholy heart could not summon his omnipotent rage

The Hieratic shrieked using all of his breath,
The stained glass immediately shattered at their feet,
There was a vile smell, a taste of death,
Nothing left but small bits of clothing, mortal remains, and his deceit

In the fetal position, he began to cower,
She was the only one who brought him rest in his darkest hour,
The only one who could tame the dark angel that preyed within,
The only one to contain his rage, his bile, his sin

From his incredible despair he fathered a black hole,
Space and time contorted according to the chaos in his soul

He once had destroyed the Heavens in rage,
Now the earth will once again pay for this heartbroken mage

The Chimera then opened his mouth for his pestilence to spread,
The Hieratic saw what he attempted to do,
Picked up the scythe and severed his head

Pandora's box now finally closed,
There was no reason to celebrate; he was once again alone

He put one of his Angel's hands to his temple and one to his heart,
A single tear fell into her right eye then streamed down his face,
He closed his eyes and began to pray

The Hieratic spoke, "Forgive me Father, your prodigal son is lost,
The purpose for this I simply do not see,
She was to be my wife, but instead my heart carries an elegy"

The Lord said, "Look at your Angel's corpse,
Call her; you'll see that she merely is sleeping,
You should understand that your love will always persevere,
Now go to your wife and stop your weeping"

The Hieratic looked at his Angel in all her unadulterated majesty,
"This is impossible, how can this be?"
"My lord it is real, please do not fear,
I am no Danaid, and desperately wish to hold you near"

Upon a nearby threshing floor, the Hieratic kissed her delicate lips,
He slowly moved his mouth to the nape of her neck,
Gingerly caressing the areola of her lustrous breasts,
They rocked back and forth in unison as he clenched her hips

His eyes locked in hers and at the moment of culmination
All time appeared to halt as the Angel's back beveled,
Suddenly there was a simultaneous exclamation,
Two hearts now beating as one, nothing short of pure revel

Wayne Fieldhouse

The sun rises on this perfect morning, the gentle breeze passing,
Here I lie in my Angel's arms,
The birds are singing and the smell of jasmine is in the air; it's just
    like a dream,
Finally freed from our bondage and all harm

"Their lives now filled with God's grace, immeasurable joy, laughter,
    and bliss,
This is no surprise, I've known this from the very start…you see, my
    name is Proteus"

For those who have been blessed to hear my word,
At times you will face challenges that seem absurd,

As the rain comes down and the cold wind blows,
Learn from my mistake,
Trust in God, turn up your collar and welcome the unknown,
I was once blind but now see, He will <u>never</u> forsake

Part II

Wayne Fieldhouse

In Her Eyes

I often lose myself in her eyes of jade,
Feeling that that was the only reason I was made

They were once filled with laughter and joy,
But my Angel believes her purpose has now been destroyed

I gently wipe her eyes and caress her delicate cheek,
Fear not my love, there are times when we all are weak

In her eyes of jade, you see,
Lies the only place I can find true tranquility

I only pray that in my heart she finds her haven,
For if she doesn't, we shall both be forsaken

Her vexed heart, troubled with endless tasks,
I will lessen them, if she simply asks

Take my hand, my love, at this cliff's end
We shall not fall, only ascend

The distance to the promised land is closer than it appears,
If we jump together, there is no need to fear

Take my words with the greatest of care,
Finally realize, that for you, I will always be there

It is her eyes of jade, alive, they keep me,
We'll overcome this arduous battle together, and finally be free

My Little Girl

As I look into the eyes of my little girl,
I see something that was lost to me,
A whole different world

A world of innocence, curiosity, and willingness to trust and learn,
Qualities that were always there, but worn away by the sands of time,
Qualities that I've only been able to subconsciously discern

It amazes me to once again see that world through your eyes,
Through experience life has hardened me and I learned to despise

Going through the various stages in your life,
You may find it perplexing, arduous, and there may be strife

Stand by my side and I'll cast the demons away,
I will be your guardian angel,
No harm will come to you I say

Every moment that I have with you, I revere,
That's because to my heart I hold you so dear

I look forward to watching you grow in profound verve,
I pray to God that I may be the father you deserve

As you grow into this beautiful woman, I want nothing more than to
    see,
That you have a fruitful life, full of tranquility

I can't wait to see your first steps,
Soon afterwards, it will appear as though all those years have leapt

And on your wedding day, to give you away, there I will be,
But realize to be truly happy, you must have your own individuality

27

Wayne Fieldhouse

Whenever you feel frustrated, hopeless and scared,
Look at this white rosebud and realize, that for you I shall always be
    there

There is no one I love more than you in this world,
That's why no matter how old you are,
To me, you'll always be my little girl

Making the Man

Awoken tonight by your cries,
Gently lifting you from your crib and holding you tight

Grabbing a blanket as we sit in my chair,
To keep us warm from the night's chilly air

You snuggle into my shoulder, the crying begins to ease,
Your mind begins to wander, then finally comes much wanted peace

Caressing your head, I look at the life I helped create in awe,
Praying I'll be able to protect you from the evil which runs wild,
I'll be right at your side every single day,
Taking care in planting the seeds of a child,
While warding off the wickedness that may blow your way

For everyone realizes we reap what we sow,
I'll use all of my will,
For my better qualities in you to show

To shower you with all of the love I can,
For the seed I plant in my child,
Will make the man

Wayne Fieldhouse

Kindred Spirits

According to legend, man was once an elated, imperial, four-legged
    beast,
Having two hearts and two souls,
The gods became infuriated to say the least

Then one day, Zeus' rancorous bolt came from the sky,
To sever the majestic beast in half,
To distribute the two souls throughout space and time

Man must now live through all of his lives,
Searching for his lost soul mate,
Hoping to find her each time before he dies

After hundreds of years I had feared my effort was futile and my ire
    became violent,
I was once a vagrant, but have finally found the path past the raging
    ocean of despair,
Yet halfway through my journey I become startled and lay silent

As I wander through my convoluted path, ahead it is Father Time I
    descry in wait,
I beg his pardon, and tell him I cannot speak now, for I am running
    late

Late to the consummation of my soul that has for centuries lain to
    bide,
The Angel across the ocean, I have finally found her; she is to be my
    bride

Looking into her verdant eyes is all I need to be nourished,
I realize my Sisyphean crusade has come to an end,
I know this is only the beginning; we will meet our ventures in life
    and flourish

With a gentle wave of his hand, my destiny came to an end,
The Angel had vanished,
I looked upon this tired old man, wishing for his death

If you had listened with all of your might,
You could actually hear my heart break,
You could see all of my hope vanish from sight

I turned to the empty sky above and beckoned your name,
Knowing that there would be no answer,
No longer any meaning to life,
No longer any reason to stay

My lamentable soul lit a fire
In the shell of my body, as its funeral pyre

Someone gently whispered in my ear, and in her voice I sensed pain
"We will be together my love, our time just isn't now; until we meet
    again"

Tears of sorrow poured from the sky above,
Extinguishing my disheartenment with her love

The empty cup that had once been my soul,
For another eternity has been made full

Your spirit is what keeps me strong,
The only reason why I've stayed alive this long

I raise my hands to my kindred spirit and bellow, "There isn't
    anything I wouldn't do,
To have you by my side in life…just to be loved by you."

Although for this there is no reason or rhyme,
Remember, true love has no fear of time

Wayne Fieldhouse

Dreams in the Darkness

My bones grew weary from my gaunt quest,
There was an old oak tree near the aged High Place,
It was time for my haggard body to rest

Moments later I awakened to see,
A regal structure in the distance,
Perhaps they could grant better shelter for me

As I trekked the alpine in front of me,
I couldn't believe my eyes,
It appeared to be an ancient chantry

As the doors slowly opened, I tried to view its inner chambers,
There was very poor light,
The smell of evil was in the air, something was not right

As I peered I saw a woman towards the candles lurch,
A sparkle coming from the altar,
Just as I had feared, it was Saint Roch's church

Turning around to flee,
The doors slammed in my face,
A tender voice said, "You mustn't leave"

With greatest apprehension I ventured down the aisle,
Atop her is a stained glass portrait of the crucifixion,
I felt the presence of God leaving me, then a sudden stench of bile

Rosary around her wrists did lie,
I've never had such fear before,
My only wish was to hie

My body forced to stay motionless, what could I do?
"I light this candle in your name," throwing it at me,
"I'm praying for you"

She turned and I gazed at a weathered face with no eyes,
Dear God this is my Angel,
How has this happened to you, why...?

With a flash of light, the portrait of Christ morphed,
An hourglass tomb it had formed,
As the sands of time fell, like a trapped animal she twisted and
    contorted

Feverishly I fumbled to break the glass,
She was no longer moving,
I looked to see each closing breath, and then, finally, her last

As the bethel became engulfed in flames,
The monks of this holy place entered,
Shouting, "He is to blame!"

With absolute fury in their eyes,
"He killed our High Priestess, for this he must die"

I ran for the first door I could see,
All of reality had been changed,
As I entered, it became Escher's "Relativity"

Frantically looking for a route to abscond,
I tried what felt to be thousands of doors,
All were locked...all but one

The writing on the doors made no sense as I passed,
Only this door had something vaguely familiar,
It looked almost like...Thurisaz?

As I entered into the room, I was surrounded by a stained glass
    portrait of Judah,
I turned and found a monk coming at me,
In our struggle I attempted to remove his cowl, but couldn't see who
    he was

Wayne Fieldhouse

Through the portrait I was propelled,
What world was this? Was I still asleep?
Was I in Hell?

Relentlessly hunted by this man,
What in God's name was happening,
I don't understand

As I fell I saw landscape in all directions infinitely expand,
There was an awkward cut on my right hand

Running through the Garden of Trepidation,
From my wounds I now grew weary,
As I rested, the ground beneath became an ossuary

Desecrated souls tore at my robe,
Scrambling with all of my might,
I'd but given up all hope
Then as they were about to deliver the fatal blow,
The monk extended his hand,
I couldn't help feel this is someone I know

He grabbed me by the throat; I quickly turned to see,
That we were somehow standing above raging waters on a
    promontory

Summoning all of the rage in my soul,
I took his feet out from under him,
You shall feel my wrath; your life will be the toll

While holding it by the hand, in the wind the cowl flailed,
It was my Angel staring at me with no eyes,
She blankly asked, "Can't you see it was me you failed"

Her face then cracked like aged plaster,
A new face emerged with blonde hair and eyes of sapphire,
A face that I knew, but could not place,
Was staring at me; all I heard was diabolical laughter

She told me to look at my wound, that's the key,
I looked at my hand and did abhor,
It was the symbol…the cursed symbol from the door

Trying to lift her I begged to be absolved from my sins,
As she started to speak, down come torrential winds

Her hand slipped from mine, as she fell to the jagged rocks below,
It felt as if time had stopped,
Her descent appeared perpetually slow

I had her in my hands…I was so close,
Will my tormented soul ever find rest?
The sun sets and my surroundings become bitterly cold,
Left with nothing to comfort me, but my dreams in the darkness

Wayne Fieldhouse

A Time Long Since Forgotten

In a time long ago, in a land far away,
Lived two children whose love for each other,
Grew stronger with the passing of every day

Soul mates they were destined to be,
Or so it had appeared,
But peace in their land was threatened,
Staring into his eyes she saw nothing but fear

A virile young boy, barely a man,
Looks back into the eyes of his true love,
And takes her by the hand

"I pledge to you this promise ring for you to always wear,
Soon I shall come, to claim you as my bride,
With God as my witness, I make this covenant,
In His name and before you, I do swear"

He was to embark upon the most paramount war of all,
With nothing more than a kiss and a warrant for her love,
Leaving his life in the hands of the Fates,
Unknowing of what was eventually to come,
How his hatred would consume him,
Leading to God's fall

An endless cycle of day turning to night and then into day,
His comrades fading with exhaustion lay dying in debris,
They were no match for the demons, just easy prey

Gillies peers the battlegrounds to see he has been forlorn,
Anger, hatred, and desperation fill his very essence,
He raises the mighty Caladbolg, and from its tip lightning cascades,
His surroundings fade to black,
Something in him was spawned that cold October day;
Some hideous force reborn

Jody Christie

229 - 4391

...is program is a pre-paid sign up in advance program)

...rlington YogaWorks is open 7 days per week.

...for both drop-in and sign-up in advance type classes.

Drop-In fee is $13.00 per class .   Phone: 845.473.9074

...ogaWorks   50 Raymond Ave. Poughkeepsie, New York 12603

Eventually he rises from the ground to see,
The demons have been destroyed,
His village was finally free

Like a wounded animal, back to his village he claws his way,
To find Little Raven, this would be their wedding day

Reaching the perimeter of his village,
Dumbfounded he simply stares,
Nothing was left, but an obscure castle,
Everything else in sight had been pillaged

At the castle gate stood the three Norns,
"Go back Gillies Macpherson, there is nothing left here for you"
He stares at each with unrivalled scorn

He advances towards the gate,
The Norns stand their ground,
"Gillies, it's too late"

Not a word he says as on he moves,
They speak in unison, "Do not cross that threshold,
It will be the end of your soul my son,
Something has happened to you, you must be told"

"Bite your tongues supercilious wenches,
For my bride through these gates I am to wed"
The Norns speak, "You cannot, for she is dead"

With a simple wave of his hand,
The Norns are thrown to the ground,
No matter how much they struggled,
They could not stand

Gillies turns to enter as they all search for something to throw,
They each find a handful of rocks,
"This will force him to regain his memory,
He has to remember…he has to know"

As he is struck in the head with a stone,
He becomes startled and a memory flashes,
Back to the time he was first left alone

To the time when his parents were persecuted for what he had done,
To the time he first discovered his powers, when he was very young

Regaining control in a swell of wrath,
He smiles as he forces two of the Norns to choke,
Leaving only one alive in the aftermath

"If you enter that gate without this word I heed,
Your life will never be the same,
Your soul will never again find peace"

Gillies looks at her with ridicule,
"I must enter these gates and find Little Raven,
She cannot be dead, I feel her presence,
You know not what you say old fool"

"So be it, you were warned,
The first person that you see,
Will be your greatest adversary,
You will find your true destiny when you defeat this foe,
For if you don't, your soul will be damned for a thousand eternities,
It is your only hope"

Gillies spat upon her face as he enters the castle gate,
Crossing the threshold he looks down to see,
The mighty Cerberus fast asleep

Everything around was covered with the dust of time,
How long had he been gone?
As he traveled these dark corridors, every candle he passed,
Started to light

Showing him the way to through the castle, to find the lake,
All mirrors have been covered in each room as he passed,
The walls began to bellow and the floor began to quake

The corridor became bitterly cold,
Up his spine ran a chill,
A powerful intuition that someone had been killed

All candles extinguish as a raging wind passes,
A light shines from as far as he can see,
"Some form of chicanery"

As he reaches the end of this apparent endless path,
He stands before a frozen lake and falls to his knees,
For what he saw he refused to believe

A woman was in a glass coffin in the center of the lake,
Adorned in a divine emerald gown and flowing scarlet hair,
Ice covered her place of rest; he was unable to clearly see her face,
It looked like his Little Raven as a woman, but where was her ring?
He took notice of his surroundings and become somewhat scared

In his haste he neglected to see,
That giant slumbering basilisks,
Were surrounding him

He slowly traces her face through the sarcophagus glass cover,
Simply staring at her, "I'm on the outside looking in,
How can this possibly be over?"

Taking his hands into his face he begins to bawl,
Something was taken from him, a part of his soul

Just at that moment a voice fell upon the wind,
A voice of a little girl that he somehow recalls,
It beckons him from the passage he left, calling him in

He looks down to see,
Bloody footprints at his feet

He glances over at his love and then lured by this little girl's laughter,
He quickly rises as not the wake the demons that sleep,
Taking great care to creep

He dashes towards the castle hoping to find,
That little girl or a clue of any kind

The footprints lead to a giant library on the castle's southern side,
Thousands of books as far as the naked eye could see,
All about magic, science, mathematics, and mythology,
He finds himself in front of a bookcase, with a bloody handprint on
the Ragnorak,
Perhaps it was a secret passage, he had to try

He pulled down the book and an inner chamber in front of him
appears,
Drawn down the damp, twisted stairs by the sound of the little girl's
tears

Carefully coming to the last step,
A shrine with a menstrual blood soaked cloth and ale stands in the
corner,
Grabbing his chest, attempting to catch his breath

He takes a nearby torch and to his surprise,
A mural of Dagda and the Morrigan consummating on the riverbed,
dances on the wall,
But something was different, something weird,
His hand was reaching for Netzcah, from the Tree of Life,
It was one of its spheres

As he encroached the orb,
Dagda's hand emerged from the bulwark,
Holding it in his mighty hand
He stopped in horror

Cautiously he moves throughout the room,
Exploring every feature,
He must find the girl soon

An enormous mirror on the far side stands erect,
Partially uncovered,
He goes over to check

As he approaches, down the burlap cover falls,
He looks to see himself and Little Raven as he had remembered her,
Covered with blood,
She was the one that called

He looks behind him to see, but she wasn't there,
"Who is performing such trickery?"

Upon further examination, everything was the same,
But the other side was decrepit and decayed,
Was he going insane?

The glass he reaches to touch with his hand,
It ripples as Little Raven pleads for his help,
"I do not understand"

Her hand against his and the promise ring he sees,
In his reflection there appears a stranger,
"My God what has happened to me?"
"Who is this before my eyes...doppelganger?"

It looks like his sword is right next to her embedded into the pillar,
Piercing something that he can't make out,
"The Jack of Diamonds...why is it piercing a card?"

Then a giant basilisk comes from out of the orb,
He reaches to his side to find his scabbard,
But there was no sword

His only route of escape was now blocked off,
He hides his eyes from the demon for fear of death,
There's only one way to live,
He dives through the mirror as he holds his breath

Wayne Fieldhouse

He opens his eyes on the other side,
The basilisk now looking directly at him,
Sees his own reflection and instantly dies of fright

"At my hands I now look,
The blood wasn't there before,
Did it rub off from the book?"

Suddenly the Morrigan appears,
He dashes for his sword to protect Little Raven,
For some reason the sword refuses its master,
His spirit fills with fear

Little Raven shouts that everything is the exact opposite on this side,
He takes the sword with his left hand,
The tarnished piece begins to brilliantly shine,
"Leave this place foul mistress, the girl is mine!"

From the corner of his eye he notices Little Raven bending to hold the
        card,
The Morrigan sees Gillies is distracted and begins to transform,
"Badb, Nemain, and the Morrigan I now stand before"

Gillies turns and finds to his surprise,
Skeptical if he would survive such a battle,
Would this adversary lead to his demise?

In a fit of rage he draws his sword,
Gallantly defending his childhood love,

The battle appeared to last quite some time,
The sun had set, it was getting late,
Both were tiring greatly, but there cannot be a stalemate

Out of the corner of the his eye,
He notices Huginn and Munnin,
Odin's spies

With a gentle nod,
They realized that he needed their help,
They each understood what had to be done

The ravens drop from above,
Clenching Badb and Nemain with their mighty talons,
Unable are they to move

At the distracted Morrigan, his sword he now points at her throat,
She speaks, "This is only the beginning you fool, I wouldn't gloat"

"You shall go throughout life cursed, you'll soon see,
Hoping to find the truth about yourself, instead you'll find your
    destiny,
All of those whom you love and find dear,
Will feel the rage you showed me today,
They will find the demon that hides within,
You will never see love in their eyes, only fear"

"And when you think you've defeated all of your foes and finally
    obtained peace,
You'll realize it's merely your beginning, and he will emerge again,
You'll never tame the beast"

"There will be one that you think can cleanse all the sins of your soul,
You will be the very source of her despair and will always be too late,
You'll go throughout your life searching for her and your absolution,
In the end the love in your heart will be consumed by your hate"

He stares at the wall as spikes transpire,
"Then in Hell I will see you my dear,
We'll both burn in a lake of fire"

He smiles as he raises his hand at a very slow pace,
Putting it near her torso and forcing her into the emerging spikes,
Until he sees them pierce her entire body and her face

He turns to look at Little Raven in woe,
He stares into her eyes as they change to a radiant sapphire,
Astonished he watches her speak,
"You will obtain peace when you find your faith,
That is all I can tell you, for this I do know"

He smiles as he puts his fingers through her hair,
She speaks, "You know what you must now do my dear"

He looks at her lovingly, "Pax copia my love",
He severs her head as she closes her eyes,
Placing her head next to her body,
He hysterically begins to cry

From her corpse spills forth light so great,
The goddesses' remains disintegrate

Weakened from his battle he returns through the mirror to the other
    side,
He senses something is again wrong, someone in the shadows trying
    to hide

The mighty Cerberus emerges from the shadows near the gateway,
Through sheer instinct he magically conjures a lyre and lulls him to
    sleep,
There shall be no more battles today

As he exits the castle he enters a land he no longer knew,
Exhaustion has taken over his body as he tumbles into the snow

Darkness begins to fill his mind,
Then an image appears,
Is it too late?
Back to a time long since forgotten,
Before his soul filled with hate

I am the Vine...

As he lay in bed, listening to the silence of the night,
When something traveled past with the wind,
A chilling voice that initially made him resonate with fright

Unable to make out what the wind had to say,
He crept from his bed to venture outside,
He knew that for this in some fashion he would pay

Against his better judgment he follows the wind's beckoning song,
Leading him to the forbidden forest,
His parents told him never to enter for in there something was wrong

As he encroaches the perimeter near the trees,
A beautiful voice now calls his name,
So lovely he instantly falls to his knees.

He slowly raises his head to see a beautiful Angel in his sight,
Standing at a fork in the road, to the left a beautiful straight path,
Turning he sees a dark, twisted trail, filled with obstacles, captivating
    him on his right

Driven by the enchanting call,
He wanders into the darkened forest,
With no fear at all

As he trudges forward, thicker becomes the brush,
His calves being cut by something that feels like thorns,
He covers his mouth with his hand, for his yelling to hush

Looking back he catches a glimpse of the Angel in his left eye,
She fondly looks at him, blows him a kiss, and begins to cry

Lightning flashes fill the sky,
From its light he now can see,
That this forest no longer has any trees

Wayne Fieldhouse

Chains hanging from the very sky itself dangle and rotate in place,
Now realizing what had been cutting his legs,
He hurriedly attempts to dodge blades heading for his face

Thousands of single twisted helixes, covered entirely with chaotically
    positioned blades,
He begins to think to himself what a tragic mistake he had made

He begins to silently pray and looks up into the cerise sky,
Something with a brilliant white/blue hue on the ground did lie

He looks to find an effulgent silver cross,
Simply sitting in the middle of this wasteland,
Whose could it be? What a terrible loss

As he touches it, he can hear the voice again,
It was so exquisite; he now heard what it had said

"I am the vine",
What does that mean?
Just as the voice finished its sentence,
Thorns began to wrap around his feet

Holding the cross upright at its base,
A sword emanated from the top,
But the reflection from the blade did not show his face

It was the face of a valiant warrior, with a mark in his left eye,
He gingerly attempts to use it against his newfound foe,
As the thorns travel up his thighs

Anger fills him, an uncontrollable rage,
The cross slips from his hand and inverts,
He catches it before it hits the ground,
It turns from silver to brass,
As the thorns travel up him, forming a cage

He's drawn to once again look at its gleaming blade,
To his demise he sees the same man, but horrid and fetid,
"Who is this man that stares into my face?"

A tree had begun to sprout in front of him when the thorns began to
    attack,
The tree appeared to be normal, but any kind of fruit it had lacked

Rain began to heavily descend,
Two people emerged from the shadows,
He prayed they were his friends

It was the fetid warrior with an alluring Harpy at his side,
There was nowhere for him to run, nowhere for him to hide

They now stand before him staring at the sword,
The Harpy bends over to whisper in his ear,
He somehow excitedly waits to hear her words

The warrior pushes her to the side,
He screams, "You are not one of His branches, for I am the vine!"

The sword retracts to cut his right hand,
He spoke, "It won't be long until you understand"

A curious shape it had made, if you could only see,
Looking at it quickly it looked similar to the letter "p"

If you could only see the pain in her eyes,
Eyes he could never have seen before,
Thinking of how he knows this woman's touch,
Then she caught him by surprise

She quickly whispers, "The key to your salvation is the circle's power
    and your faith."
She passionately kisses him and roughly holds him by the face

Wayne Fieldhouse

With her index finger nail,
She slits his throat,
He notices something on her hand with the same color shine,
Just before his body had failed

As he's dying her voice he can hear,
"The power of the circle is insurmountable,
Find it and it will eliminate your darkest fears"

About the Author

Wayne Fieldhouse is 31 years old, and currently works in the field of pharmaceuticals. He holds both Bachelor's and Master's degrees in Chemical Engineering from the New Jersey Institute of Technology.

Wayne's interest in mythology and folklore started at a very young age. These stories lay dormant in his mind until one day, as a joke, he and a few of his friends began to play with an Ouija® board. The piece mysteriously flew under his fingertips and revealed that he had been a great wizard long ago – a man who fought for good, but was forever haunted by his dark inner being; a man who also struggled to find his kindred spirit. This joke spawned a raging eagre of thoughts that soon became the Heretic. "Sometimes distant worlds are not so far away," explains the author.

Wayne resides in New Jersey with his wife, Laurie, his daughter, Ashley, and his son, Ryan.

Printed in the United States
24835LVS00001B/191

9 781410 779052